CONTENTS

Some words are shown in bold, **like this**. You can find out what they mean by looking in the glossary.

BE A FILM-MAKER!

Film-makers work with cameras, **scripts**, actors, **props**, and music to create film magic. If you dream about making films of your own, you could become a film-maker!

Dream It, Do It!

GET FILMING!

Mary Colson

Raintree

Raintree is an imprint of Capstone Global Library Limited, a company incorporated in England and Wales having its registered office at 7 Pilgrim Street, London, EC4V 6LB – Registered company number: 6695582

www.raintreepublishers.co.uk
myorders@raintreepublishers.co.uk

Text © Capstone Global Library Limited 2014
First published in hardback in 2014
The moral rights of the proprietor have been asserted.

Edited by Rebecca Rissman, Dan Nunn, and Helen Cox Cannons
Designed by Steve Mead
Original illustrations © Capstone Global Library 2014
Picture research by Ruth Blair
Production by Vicki Fitzgerald
Originated by Capstone Global Library Ltd
Printed and bound in China

ISBN 978 1 406 27263 5
17 16 15 14 13
10 9 8 7 6 5 4 3 2 1

British Library Cataloguing in Publication Data
A full catalogue record for this book is available from the British Library.

Acknowledgements

We would like to thank the following for permission to reproduce photographs: Alamy pp.5 (© Photos 12), 25 (© AF archive); Capstone Publishers pp. 26–29 (© Karon Dubke); Corbis pp. 12 (© Mark Rightmire/ZUMA Press), 16 (© Etienne George/Sygma); Getty Images pp. 6 (Radius Images), 13 (Betsie Van der Meer), 14 (WireImage), 23 (Siri Stafford); Shutterstock pp. 4 (© Klemzy), 8 (© Khakimullin Aleksandr), 9 (© vovan), 10 left (© Albert Ziganshin), 10 right (© David Evison), 11 (© Yuri Arcurs), 15 left (© van Ponomarev), 15 right (© ppart), 17 left (© pichayasri), 17 right (© Christos Georghiou), 18 (© Strejman), 19 (© Goodluz), 20 (© absolut), 20, 21 (© ostill). Incidental photographs reproduced with permission of Shutterstock.

Cover photograph of a boy holding a video camera reproduced with permission of Corbis (© David Deas/DK Stock).

We would like to thank Chris and Kristen Barker for their invaluable help in the preparation of this book.

Every effort has been made to contact copyright holders of material reproduced in this book. Any omissions will be rectified in subsequent printings if notice is given to the publisher.

Disclaimer

All the Internet addresses (URLs) given in this book were valid at the time of going to press. However, due to the dynamic nature of the Internet, some addresses may have changed, or sites may have changed or ceased to exist since publication. While the author and publisher regret any inconvenience this may cause readers, no responsibility for any such changes can be accepted by either the author or the publisher.

Film-makers are creative, imaginative, and want to tell good stories. You can make a film about anything you like. It doesn't have to be a made-up story – you could create a film about a typical day in your life.

FILM YOURSELF

Film-makers tell stories that they hope people will want to see. What do you think would make a good story? Thinking about your own life may give you some good ideas.

Activity

Stand in front of a mirror and pretend you are looking into a camera lens. You can pretend to be someone famous, someone you know, or you can be yourself. Watch how your face moves and changes as you speak.

MOVIE MIND MAPPING

What kinds of films do you enjoy? Comedy? Action? Fantasy? Film-makers always start with an idea of the type of film they want to make and then work from there. After recording their ideas, film-makers think about how to make the story as exciting and entertaining as possible.

Activity

Start a film-maker's **journal** and note down all your brilliant story and character ideas. Don't cross any ideas out – they might be useful later!

Ideas

set at school?
sports club?
tough coach?
injury?
team win?
celebrations!

PLOTTING PLOTS

All films need a good **plot**, or story. What's your plot going to be? Is it going to be about good winning over evil? Or about someone solving a problem and learning something important? A film-maker plots out every detail of his or her film.

Activity

Imagine you're planning a film with a hero and a baddie in it. Plan out your plot by answering the following questions in your **journal**.

1. Where and when does your story take place?
2. Who is your hero?
3. Who is your baddie?
4. What happens when they meet?

WRITING THE SCRIPT

All films have **scripts**. Scripts tell the actors and actresses what to say and where to stand. They also describe a **scene**, or place, where the action happens.

Activity

Have a script reading! Ask an adult to help you find the script of a film you like. Get your friends to read different parts out loud.

A script reading with friends can be fun.

CHARACTERS, COSTUMES, AND CASTING

Film-makers need to choose the right characters for their film and to dress them in the right way. For example, evil characters often wear black, and good characters wear white.

Voldemort, Harry Potter Films

Activity

Draw outlines of people in your **journal**. Create a **collage** of your characters by cutting out pictures from magazines. Think about how you want them to look and the clothes they should wear. It might help you to think of which real-life actors and actresses you would **cast** to play your characters.

ON LOCATION: SET DESIGN

Some film-makers build **sets**, or stages. Others film outdoors, or in famous places. Where do you want your film set? In a forest? In a new world? In a castle? Think creatively!

Activity

Take a cardboard box and cut away one side. Gather together card, paint, and pens and create a mini set!

Using cut-out figures (or dolls) as your characters, move them around the set as you speak their lines. Which part of the set works best?

MUSIC AND ATMOSPHERE

Music is used in films to create different moods and emotions. Think about scary moments in films – such as a shark attack – where the music adds to the **atmosphere**.

Activity

Choose five pieces of music that you think create different moods, such as scary, happy, or sad. Make a **soundtrack** of these five pieces.

Play your pieces to a friend. Ask them how the music makes them feel. Do they agree with you?

CAMERAS AND ANGLES

We don't always see film action from the same angle. Sometimes, we see the view from above and sometimes we see a **close-up**. Film-makers experiment with different camera angles to keep the audience interested.

Activity

Use a camera to practise zooming in on an object. If you don't have a camera, use your hands to make an imaginary lens to look through. Try filming the object from above, the side, and below.

FILMING AND EDITING

Film-makers make their movies and then **edit** them. Editing is when bits of the film are pieced together or cut out, or a camera angle might be changed. This is to make the best film possible for the audience to enjoy.

Activity

After you've finished filming a **scene**, watch it back. Do you need all of it or can you cut bits out?

Show your film to an audience. What is their opinion? What changes do they suggest?

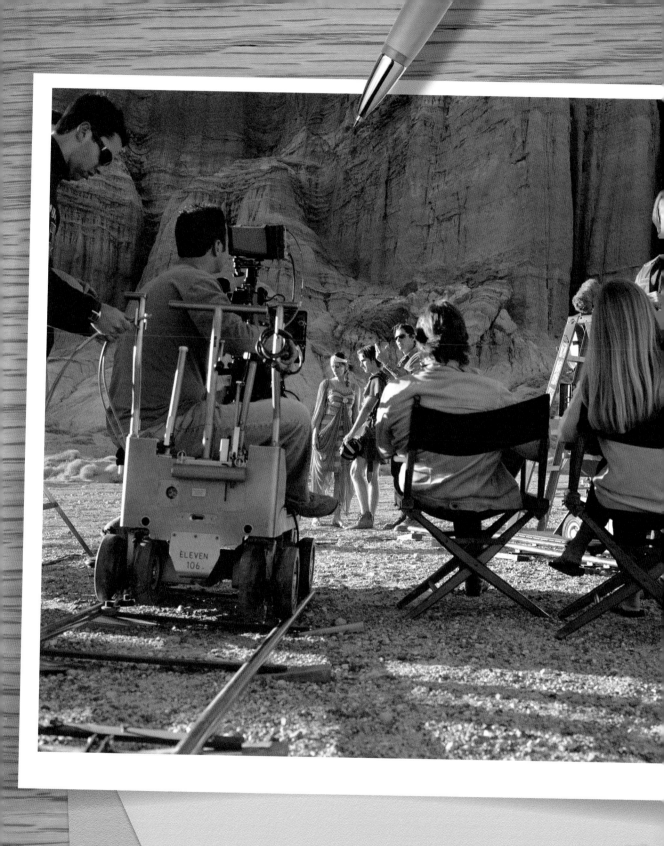

MAKING A TRAILER

All films have trailers. Trailers are short adverts for the film that are shown to audiences. The film-maker hopes that the audience will be hooked and want to see the whole film.

Activity

Choose three key moments from your film. Use these moments to make your trailer. Don't forget to show or say what the film is called and when it will be ready to watch.

Show your trailer to an audience. Are they hooked? Do they want to see the whole film?

LIGHTS, CAMERA...

A **storyboard** shows the story action **scene** by scene in pictures and notes. Film-makers use storyboards to help them track the details of the story as they film. Follow these simple steps to help you create your own film storyboard.

1. Get a large piece of paper, a ruler, and a pencil.

2. Draw eight boxes in two rows of four, one row on top of the other.

3. Rule a line either above or below each row of boxes. This will be your box for notes on each picture.

... ACTION!

4. Now you're ready to create!

5. In the first box, draw your first **scene**. Think about the setting, the time of day, and the characters in it.

6. Add any notes about what the characters are saying in the little box below the picture.

7. Do this for every box until your story is told.

8. If you like, you can colour in your picture to show the mood of the scene.

GLOSSARY

atmosphere mood or feel of your work

cast choose an actor or actress to play a part in a film

close-up zoomed-in view of something

collage picture made by sticking different materials and pictures onto paper

edit piece together, cut, or change part of a film

journal written record of a person's thoughts and experiences

plot storyline of a book, play, or film

prop object that actors and actresses use to help tell a story

scene place or setting where part of a film happens

script written words of a film

set scenery for a film

soundtrack music chosen to be used in a film

storyboard outline of a film in pictures

FIND OUT MORE

Books

Action! Making Movies, Sarah Garza, (Teacher Created Materials, 2013)

Movie Maker: The Ultimate Guide to Making Films, Tim Grabham, Suridh Hassan, Dave Reeve, and Clare Richards (Templar Publishing, 2010)

Websites

www.minimoviemakers.com/index.html
Ask an adult to help you use this site. Watch clips of videos and learn cool tips for your next movie.

INDEX